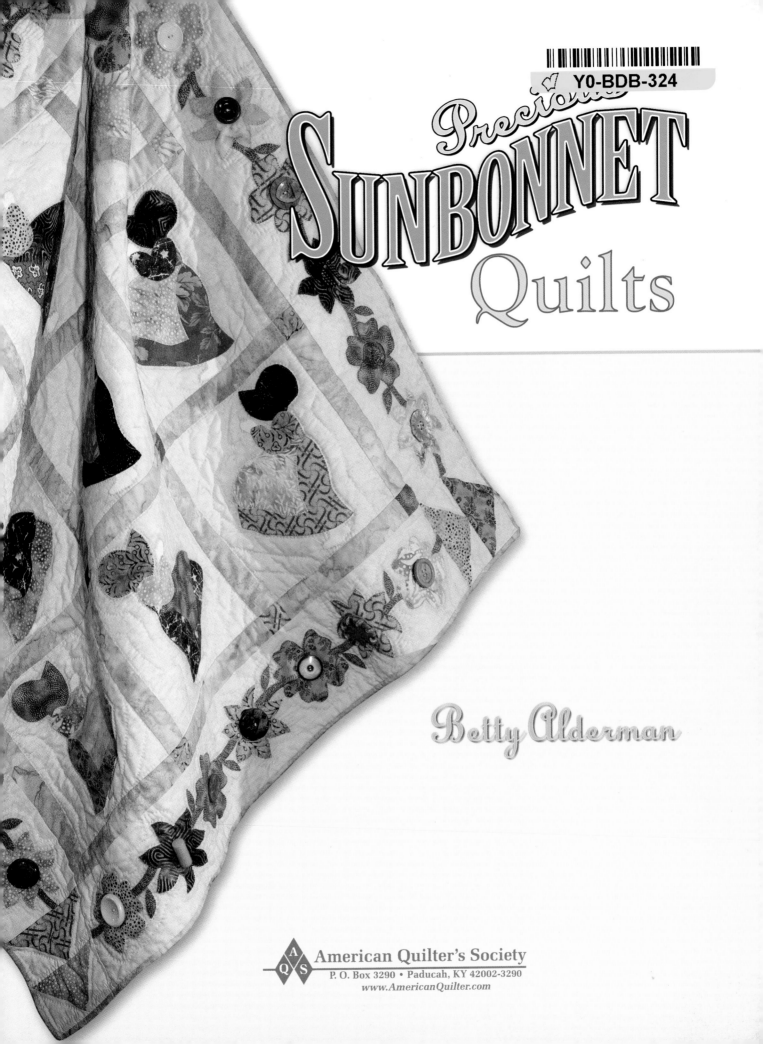

Precious SUNBONNET Quilts

Betty Alderman

American Quilter's Society
P. O. Box 3290 • Paducah, KY 42002-3290
www.AmericanQuilter.com

Located in Paducah, Kentucky, the American Quilter's Society (AQS) is dedicated to promoting the accomplishments of today's quilters. Through its publications and events, AQS strives to honor today's quiltmakers and their work and to inspire future creativity and innovation in quiltmaking.

Text © 2008, Author, Betty Alderman
Artwork © 2008, American Quilter's Society

Executive Editor: Nicole C. Chambers
Editor: Jennifer Lokey
Graphic Design: Elaine Wilson
Cover Design: Michael Buckingham
Photography: Charles R. Lynch
Illustrations: Betty Alderman

American Quilter's Society
P. O. Box 3290 • Paducah, KY 42002-3290
www.AmericanQuilter.com

Additional copies of this book may be ordered from the American Quilter's Society, PO Box 3290, Paducah, KY 42002-3290, or online at www.AmericanQuilter.com.

Library of Congress Cataloging-in-Publication Data

Alderman, Betty.
  Precious sunbonnet quilts / by Betty Alderman.
     p. cm.
  ISBN 978-1-57432-951-3
  1. Appliqué--Patterns. 2. Quilting--Patterns. 3. Quilts. I. Title.

  TT779.A39 2008
  746.44'5041--dc22

                              2008007020

Proudly printed and bound in the United States of America

DEDICATION

In memory of my mother,
Ada Touchstone Waples, 1894–1985.
   You gave me pencil and paper and needle and thread and then
you praised what I did with them. I am eternally grateful.

ACKNOWLEDGMENTS

Thank you to the American Quilter's Society for having confidence in my ability to put together a book of patterns featuring, the sometimes controversial, Sunbonnet Sue. By publishing this book, you have helped me keep this delightful icon of American quilting alive for future generations.

I owe a big debt of gratitude to my daughter, Betsy Lewis. You are always willing to help me get my writing organized and into my computer; plus your special interest in the Sunbonnet Babies' creator, Bertha Corbett, has inspired me to perpetuate her legacy.

To Fred Alderman. You work so diligently at providing a perfect environment so that I can do what I do. You are the perfect helpmate.

To the editors at AQS. Working with you all has been a delight.

Contents

PREFACE

Who among us has not made the acquaintance of Sunbonnet Sue and her little sisters, the Sunbonnet Babies? For some, it was love at first sight, while others have taken a more skeptical view of these little girls hiding behind their big hats. For the past 15 years I have drawn and stitched dozens of Sunbonnet Sues and her baby sisters, hoping to delight their loyal friends and to win over the others.

I am fascinated by the number of quilters who react strongly to the notion of Sunbonnet Sue. Although most people take delight in Sue, I am aware that there are those who turn up their noses at Sunbonnet Sue and her quilts. Several years ago I was working in a quilt shop in Arizona when a customer, upon viewing a display of Sunbonnet quilt blocks, informed me that she was a member of a quilt guild in another state and that "they" didn't like Sunbonnet Sue. Since that day, I have made it my mission to design Sunbonnet quilts that would overcome that silly kind of rejection.

No one knows exactly when the first Sunbonnet figure appeared on a quilt, but it is evident that in the 1880s Kate Greenaway drawings of little girls in big bonnets were beginning to appear on embroidered, crazy quilts. Around 1900, Bertha Corbett, a young artist living and working in Minneapolis, drew charming pictures of children in sunbonnets performing various everyday activities. She referred to her creations as the Sunbonnet Babies and it is believed that her intention was to demonstrate that the human figure could convey various moods and attitudes without the facial expressions being exposed. If that challenge was true then Bertha Corbett certainly succeeded. Credit should also be given to Bernhardt Wall, who designed Sunbonnet figures in the early years of the 20th century. Both Corbett and Wall designs could be found on various articles of the day, such as household items and paper goods. It can be surmised that needle artists of that period, looking for design ideas for their popular redwork embroidery, traced and embroidered the readily available Sunbonnet designs. Transferring the designs to appliqué was surely the next progression.

What happened to the charming, expressive little girls as they traveled onto the quilts of the 1930s and 40s? Styles changed and in the 1930s surface design reflected the popular art deco influence of the period. Sunbonnet Sue succumbed to this trend and she was transformed into the rather blockish, unadorned figure some quilters began to disdain. In 1992, after my encounter with the lady who didn't mind telling me she and her friends didn't like Sunbonnet Sue, I decided to give Sue a makeover. I took Sue under my wing and provided her with a new wardrobe, a bit more attitude, sometimes sweet, sometimes jaunty.

Some of the designs in this book are my favorites from over the past 15 years, but now she has wonderful new fabrics for her outfits and exciting new settings for her quilts. Others are new creations for the 21st century. At heart, though, she is the same darling Sunbonnet that our great-grandmothers cherished more than 100 years ago.

INTRODUCTION

This book is a tribute to a friend of mine, Sunbonnet Sue. She and I have enjoyed each other's company for almost 20 years. I first made her acquaintance at Laurene Sinema's quilt shop, The Quilted Apple. The shop was featuring Sunbonnet Sue as a *block-of-the-month* theme and I decided to make a Sunbonnet quilt for my little granddaughter, Jessica. Several years later I produced my first commercial pattern, Sunbonnet Calendar Girls. Since then, Sue and I have been traveling together, making new friends at quilt shows and teaching venues all over the country. Through the pages of this book we hope you will come to know us better and enjoy our company, as well.

Betty

General INSTRUCTIONS

Before you begin work on any of the quilts in this book, read through these General Instructions and the instructions for each project. Every effort has been made to help you, the quiltmaker, have an enjoyable and stress-free experience as you stitch your quilt to completion. The directions are written for the quiltmaker who possesses basic quiltmaking skills. The quilts are simply constructed and should not challenge the advanced beginner or intermediate quiltmaker.

The quilts in this book have been appliquéd using lightweight, paper-backed fusible web as a bonding agent. On some quilts the edges of the appliqué have been finished by machine, and on others the edges are finished by hand. You can choose the method you prefer. In all cases, either method will add a lovely detail to your work.

All the seam allowances are ¼" and are included in the cutting measurements. All border measurements are given. However, since individual quilts vary slightly, it is suggested that you measure your quilt as you add the borders to determine the exact length of each border, indicated by the measurements of your individual quilt.

Directions for Fusible-Web Appliqué

❖ Before you begin, read the directions below and the directions included with the fusible web.

❖ Prepare your background pieces by cutting and pressing. You will want to cut your background a little larger than called for, since the appliqué and stitching may distort the background fabric. Trim the background to the correct size after the appliqué is complete.

❖ With your #2 pencil, trace each design element onto the paper side of the fusible web, leaving at least ½" between each design element.

❖ Cut the designs out, leaving a small margin beyond the drawn line.

❖ Set your dry iron to the wool setting. This is important, as too hot an iron will melt the glue and it will not adhere to the fabric.

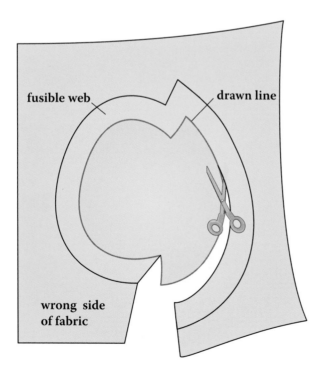

Cut out the designs along the drawn line.

❖ Press each design onto the **wrong** side of the chosen appliqué fabric. Press for about 4 seconds.

❖ Cut out the designs along the drawn line as shown.

❖ Peel the paper backing from the appliqué designs. When you have peeled off the paper backing, the back of the fabric should have a shiny look. Place the appliqué piece, shiny or wrong-side down, onto the right side of the background fabric. It is helpful to make a tracing of the design and place it on top of the appliqué. This will act as a placement guide. Check to be sure every piece is in the position you want it to be in. A very scant overlap, about the width of 3 threads, is all that is needed when placing one appliqué piece over another.

❖ Remove the tracing guide and press the appliqué for about 4 seconds. Turn the block over and press again on the back for 4 seconds.

❖ Using the method you prefer, stitch around the edges of the appliqué. See the sections on Machine- or Hand-Stitched Fusible Appliqué.

Machine-Stitched Fusible Appliqué

After the appliqué pieces have been fused to the background, you are ready to machine stitch around the edges of the appliqué.

❖ Before you begin, make sure your machine is clean and in good running order. Dust around the bobbin case and feed dogs.

❀ Place a new needle in your machine.

❀ Select the stitch you will be using. Most likely you will use a buttonhole stitch or a zigzag stitch, but any swing stitch will do.

❀ Depending on the look you prefer, choose a thread that either matches or contrasts nicely with the appliqué.

❀ Fill several bobbins with matching thread.

❀ Make a sample before you begin. This will help you find the right tension, stitch length and width. If your work is puckering, you will need to use a stabilizer. Paper toweling will work well as a stabilizer. Place it between your background fabric and the feed dogs. Tear away the stabilizer after your stitching is complete.

❀ Stitch in place for several stitches and then set your stitch to the desired setting. The stitch should go into the background fabric at the outside edge of the appliqué and then swing onto the appliqué piece. When you are finished, stitch in place, again, for several stitches. Clip threads close to the last stitches.

❀ Machine appliqué is like any decorative stitching. It takes practice and patience but the effort is rewarding and well worth the effort to learn. Visit your local quilt shop to find a variety of quilt books devoted to machine appliqué.

Hand-Stitched Fusible Appliqué

Buttonhole stitching, by hand, around the fused appliqué is a beautiful way to complete your appliqué.

❀ Choose embroidery floss in a color that will complement your fabric. It can either match or contrast, depending on the effect you desire.

❀ Thread a #8 embroidery needle with 2 strands of embroidery floss. The floss should be about 18" in length. A longer thread will tangle and become frayed.

❀ Start your stitching by using the waste-knot method shown in the sidebar

Waste-Knot Method

Thread your embroidery needle with the required number of strands and make a knot.

With your needle on top of your work, stab the needle into the right side of your fabric about 2" away from your starting point.

Bring the needle up from the wrong side to the right side at the starting point and start to embroider.

When you are finished with this thread, weave it through several stitches on the back and clip it off.

Now cut away the knot that is on top and thread the needle with the 2" of thread. Weave this thread through several stitches on the back and clip off the remaining thread.

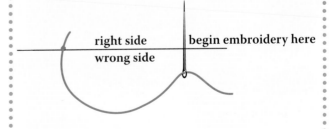

right side | begin embroidery here
wrong side

❖ When finishing or starting a new thread, weave it under the previous threads on the back.

❖ Stitch around each appliqué piece, using the buttonhole stitch as shown on page 15.

❖ Begin by bringing your needle up next to the outside edge of the appliqué piece and stitching down into the appliqué, catching about ¼" of the appliqué fabric. Continue in this manner until all exposed edges are stitched over.

Completing Your Quilt

❖ After your quilt top is complete, press your work on the right and wrong side. Snip all the dark threads so they will not show through on the right side.

❖ Make a sandwich of your quilt top by laying your backing face down on a flat surface. Lay the batting on top of the backing, making sure it is smooth. Place the quilt top, face up, on top of the other two layers. The batting and backing should extend at least 2" beyond the quilt top. Baste the three layers together, using a long basting stitch or rustproof safety pins, placed about 5" apart. You will find quilting suggestions included in the directions for each quilt.

Mitered Corners for Binding

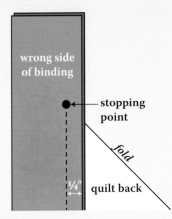

Turn the seam allowance toward the quilt back and press. Fold the quilt with the binding edges right sides together.

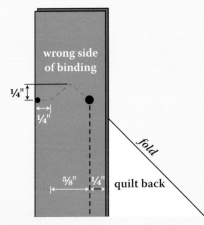

Sew as shown.

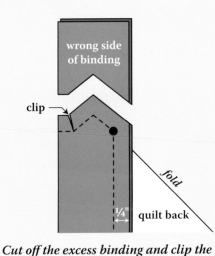

Cut off the excess binding and clip the seam allowances.

Binding Your Quilt

Yardage is given in each supply list for binding.

❧ Cut or make two strips, 1⅛" x the width of the quilt, plus 5".

❧ Cut or make two strips, 1⅛" x the length of the quilt, plus 5".

❧ Center the binding on the sides of the quilt, right sides together and the raw edges matching. The strips will extend about 2½" beyond the top and bottom of the quilt edge. Start stitching ¼" in from the top edge and stitch to within ¼" of the bottom.

❧ Repeat, until all four strips have been sewn onto the edges of the quilt.

❧ Refer to the Mitered Corners for Binding figures in the sidebar.

❧ Turn the binding towards the back of the quilt. Turn under ¼" and whipstitch in place as shown.

Whipstitch

Making a Label

After all the love and work you have put into your quilt, you will want to make a label for it. Decide on the information you want to include on the label before you decide on the size. Generally, you will want to include your name, the year, the name of your quilt and any other information you think will be of interest to someone viewing your quilt.

I admire labels that have been designed to coordinate with the quilt it identifies but, I must confess, my labels are pretty simple.

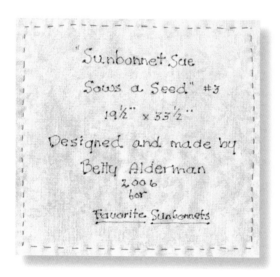

❖ Practice writing the information you will include, so that you can judge the size of the label.

❖ Cut your fabric to fit the information, adding ¼" seam allowance.

❖ Press a piece of freezer paper, shiny side down, onto the back of the fabric for stabilization.

❖ Using a permanent pen, write your information onto the fabric.

❖ Remove the freezer paper and heat set the writing on the label with a warm iron.

❖ Turn in ¼" seam allowance. With 2 strands of embroidery floss, use a running stitch to secure the label to the lower left-hand corner of the quilt. Refer to Embroidery Stitches on page 15.

Supplies to Have on Hand

Whether we devote our time and energy to making a small wallhanging or a full-size quilt, in order to achieve satisfactory results we want to use the very best tools and materials available. Nothing is more frustrating than having scissors that grab, a sewing machine that is cranky, or flimsy material. Generally speaking, we quilt for our own enjoyment and the pleasure it will give others. We can only enjoy what we are doing and love the results if we start off on the right foot with quality equipment.

Buy the best your budget will allow and you have already set the stage for a successful result.

Fabric

All of the quilts in this book were made of 100 percent cotton, purchased at shops devoted primarily to quilting supplies. By doing this I was confident that I was getting the best fabric available. I generally do not wash my fabric before I use it, but that is a personal preference. An exception to this is when I am working with red fabric. I will test it for color fastness and wash it if there is any evidence that it will run. If you are more comfortable washing your fabric before putting it into a quilt, by all means, do it.

Embroidery Stitches

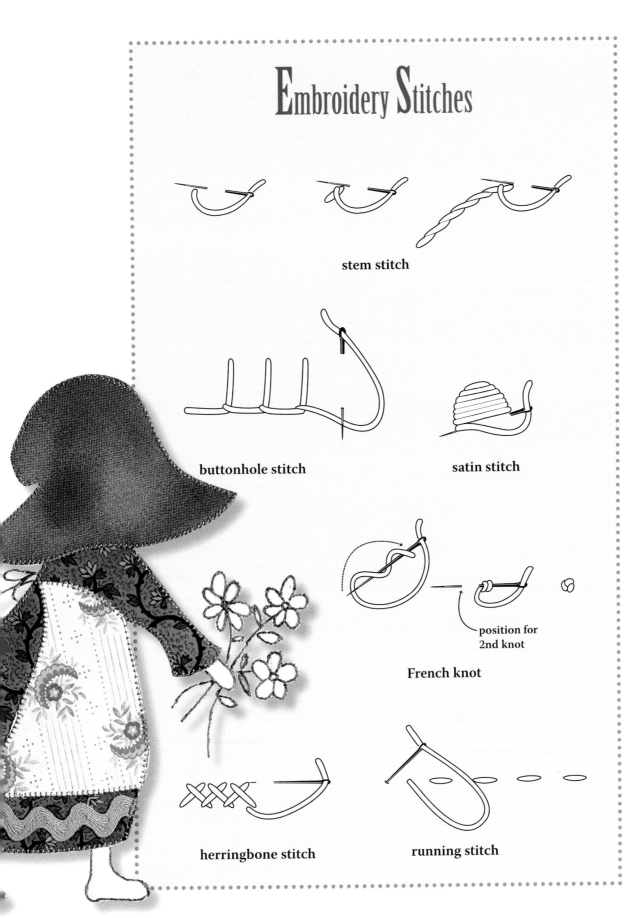

stem stitch

buttonhole stitch

satin stitch

position for
2nd knot

French knot

herringbone stitch

running stitch

Fusible Web

The appliqué on the quilts in this book was all done with lightweight, paper-backed, fusible web. Be sure to purchase "paper-backed" fusible web.

Thread

You will want to use good quality 100 percent cotton sewing machine thread for most of your piecing. Gray is a good color choice, as it will blend nicely with most fabrics.

Decorative, machine embroidery, including the buttonhole stitch, can be done using an array of luscious colors available in cotton and synthetics. Try different ones to achieve various effects.

Cotton embroidery floss is a good choice for any hand embroidery. I am often asked what color I use. I suggest picking a color that works well with the fabric in the quilt. Even redwork embroidery can be done in any red—there is no right red for redwork.

Batting

Picking the right batting can be intimidating. Numerous articles have been written about the different types on the market and there are many good ones to choose from.

Here is a rule of thumb that will make it easier to choose. If your quilt is to be machine quilted, pick a thin batting with 80% or more natural fiber. If your quilt is to be hand quilted, choose a low-loft polyester batting.

Tools for Finishing Your Quilts

- ❖ Zigzag sewing machine for machine appliqué

- ❖ Embroidery needles, size 7 or 8, for hand-finished appliqué

- ❖ Thimble for handwork

- ❖ Sharp scissors are very important! I suggest four pair: one for fabric, one for paper, one for fusible-web appliqué, and one for embroidery.

- ❖ Disposable, #2 mechanical pencil

- ❖ Tracing paper for reversing designs

- ❖ Light box (optional, but I can't live without one)

- ❖ Embroidery hoop (optional)

PROJECTS

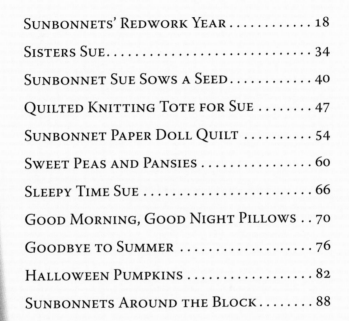

SUNBONNETS' REDWORK YEAR
30½" x 41¼"

Sunbonnets' Redwork Year

The designs for this quilt started out as miniature appliqué patterns, but I thought they would be perfect for redwork embroidery as well. As an added delight, I've included Alternate Vintage Sunbonnet patterns as well. Whether you choose to give your redwork the vintage look or go for the more traditional, I do know that you'll have fun embroidering this charming quilt. It's a really fun and easy project to share with your daughter or granddaughter.

Sunbonnets' Redwork Year
30½" x 41¼"

Supply List:

Note: Yardage is based on fabric that is at least 40" wide.

¾ yd. light background fabric

1 yd. floral fabric for sashing and outer border

¼ yd. fabric for inner border fabric

½ yd. fabric for corner squares and binding

½ yd. lightweight, paper-backed fusible web

3 skeins red, DMC® floss (Sample was done in DMC 498)

Embroidery needle, #7

#2 pencil

35" x 45" batting

35" x 45" backing – 1⅓ yds.

Cutting Measurements:

I always cut my background a little larger than called for because the appliqué and stitching may shrink the background slightly. Trim the pieces to size after the stitching is complete.

Background
12 rectangles, 6" x 7"

Sashing
9 strips, 1¾" x 6"

2 strips, 1¾" x 30¼"

Inner border
2 strips, 1¾" x 19½" (top and bottom)

2 strips, 1¾" x 32¾" (sides)

Outer border
2 strips, 4¾" x 22" (top and bottom)

2 strips, 4¾" x 32¾" (sides)

Corner squares
4 squares, 4¾" x 4¾"

Sunbonnets' Redwork Year quilt layout

Fussy cut around flower motifs.

Directions:

1. Sew the embroidery designs (pages 22–33) onto the background rectangles:

a. Using the #2 pencil, trace each design onto the 12 background rectangles.

b. Thread the embroidery needle with 2 strands of embroidery floss. Use a stem stitch to complete each design. See Embroidery Stitches, page 15.

c. Press each completed block on the wrong side.

2. Stitch the blocks, sashing, and borders together, referring to the quilt layout.

3. Create the corner fusible applique:

a. Following the manufacturer's directions, press the fusible web to the back of some of the floral border fabric.

b. Fussy cut around some of the floral motifs as shown left. Fuse these flowers over part of the seam where the border and corner blocks are stitched together. Refer to the quilt picture for approximate placement.

4. Refer to pages 12–14 for finishing details.

Quilting Suggestion

This quilt was hand quilted in the ditch around the embroidered blocks and around each redwork figure. The borders were machine quilted in a meandering fashion and in the ditch between the borders.

January

Alternate Design

Redwork

Redwork

February

Alternate Design

March

Alternate Design

Redwork

Redwork

April

Alternate Design

May

Alternate Design

Redwork

Redwork

June

Alternate Design

July

Alternate Design

Redwork

Redwork

August

Alternate Design

Alternate Design

September

Redwork

Redwork

October

Alternate Design

November

Alternate Design

Redwork

Redwork

December

Alternate Design

SISTERS SUE
24" x 24"

SISTERS SUE

I recently took a watercolor class and this quilt is a result of a small painting I did. I was experimenting with mixing colors and I found I could match up the colors of my painting with fabrics from my stash. I encourage you to do the same. Even if you don't do your own painting, try matching fabrics with a favorite picture in your home. You might be surprised how easy it is to find a pleasing color combination.

SISTERS SUE
24" x 24"

Supply List:

Note: Yardage is based on fabric that is at least 40" wide.

1 yd. center block, outer border and binding fabric
½ yd. center block triangle fabric
⅜ yd. inner border fabric
⅜ yd. outer swag fabric
¼ yd. inner swag fabric
Additional scraps for the appliqué
28" x 28" batting
28" x 28" backing – ⅞ yd.

1½ yds. lightweight, paper-backed, fusible web
Machine thread for finishing the appliqué by machine or
Embroidery floss for finishing by hand
Black, fine line, permanent marker

Cutting Measurements

I always cut my background a little larger than called for because the appliqué and stitching may shrink the background slightly. Trim the pieces to size after the stitching is complete.

BACKGROUND
1 square, 10½" x 10½"

TRIANGLES (PALE GREEN)
2 squares, 9½" x 9½" Cut these in half, diagonally, to form 4 triangles (Fig. 1, page 36).

INNER BORDER (LIGHT BLUE)
4 strips, 2½" x 26"

OUTER BORDER
4 strips, 3½" x 26"

BINDING
3 strips, 1⅛" x 40"

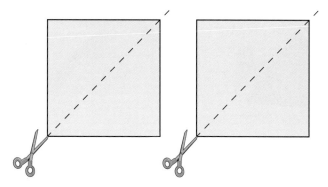

Fig. 1. *Cut each square in half to form 2 triangles from each square.*

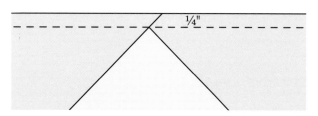

Fig. 2. *Allowing a generous ¼" margin.*

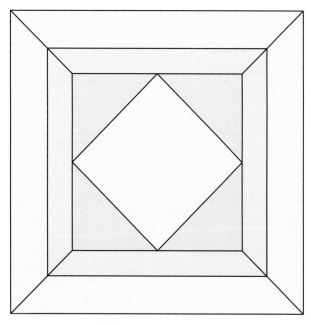

SISTERS SUE quilt layout

Directions

1. Appliqué the center background square:

a. Using the method you prefer or referring to the Directions for Fusible-Web Appliqué (pages 10–12), appliqué the 3 Sister Sue figures (pages 38–39) onto the center block.

b. Using the black, permanent pen, add the hand and details.

2. Construct the wall quilt:

a. Stitch the long edges of the 4 center block triangles to each of the sides of the center block square. Trim to form a square measuring approximately 14½" x 14½", allowing a generous ¼" margin beyond the points of the center block (Fig. 2).

b. Make 4 pairs of inner/outer border units by stitching a long edge of each inner border to the long edge of each outer border. Press seams open.

c. Attach the border units to the center of the quilt, stitching the inner border edges to the quilt center. Start and stop stitching ¼" from each end.

d. Complete the mitered corners, referring to the sidebar on page 37.

3. Appliqué the inner and outer swags onto the borders and add the tulip motifs.

4. Refer to pages 12–14 for finishing details.

Mitered Corners

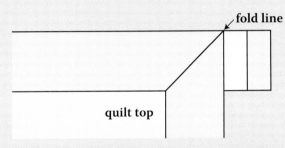

With the quilt right side up, turn the seam allow-ances toward the quilt top.

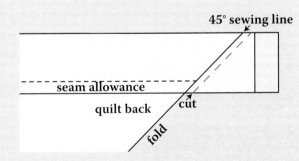

Fold the top border strip at a 45° angle, right sides together, pressing the fold to make a distinct line.

Fold the quilt top in half so the border edges are right sides together. Sew on the 45° fold line. Cut away the excess border ½" for the sewing line.

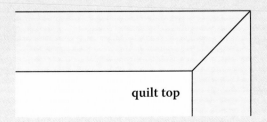

Fold back and press the mitered corner.

Quilting Suggestion

This quilt was quilted by machine, with stitching in the ditch and using a meandering pattern in the quilt center. The borders were stitched in a loop and circle design.

place on fold

40

SUNBONNET SUE *Sows a Seed*

Sunbonnet Sue planting her garden is a recurring theme in my Sunbonnet quilts. In fact, one of the first quilts I ever designed for a class at The Quilted Apple in Phoenix was such a quilt. I hope you enjoy my new version—it even has some dimensional flowers you can plant in the borders!

SUNBONNET SUE SOWS A SEED
19½" x 39"

Supply List

NOTE: Yardage is based on fabric that is at least 40" wide.

- ¼ yd. light background
- ¼ yd. sashing and leaf appliqué
- ½ yd. inner border and appliqué
- ½ yd. red print for outer side border, binding, and appliqué
- ¼ yd. green print for outer side border and appliqué
- ⅛ yd. of 2 different light prints for top and bottom borders and appliqué
- Additional red and green scraps for corner blocks and appliqué

- 2 yds. lightweight, paper-backed fusible web for appliqué
- ½ yd. jumbo rickrack for dress trim
- 1 skein dark green embroidery floss to coordinate with fabrics
- Matching machine thread for finishing appliqué by machine or
- Matching embroidery floss for finishing appliqué by hand
- Embroidery needle, # 8
- Ten ⅝" buttons for flower centers
- 24" x 43" batting
- 24" x 43" backing – 1¼ yds.
- #4 pencil

Cutting Measurements

I always cut my background a little larger than called for because the appliqué and stitching may shrink the background slightly. Trim the pieces to size after the stitching is complete.

BACKGROUND

3 rectangles, 8" x 9"

SASHING

4 strips, 1¼" x 8"

2 strips, 1¼" x 29"

INNER BORDER

2 strips, 3" x 9½" for the top and bottom

2 strips, 3" x 34" for sides

OUTER BORDER

3" x 14½" (1st light print) top

3" x 14½" (2nd light print) bottom

3" x 34" (red print) side

3" x 34" (green print) side

CORNER SQUARES

4 squares, 3" x 3" from red and green scraps

SUNBONNET SUE SOWS A SEED *quilt layout*

Directions

1. Appliqué blocks with embroidery:

a. Using the method you prefer or referring to the Directions for Fusible-Web Appliqué (pages 10–12), appliqué the Sunbonnet Sue designs (pages 44–46) onto the 3 background rectangles. The central figure can be reversed to match the original quilt. Permission is granted to do this at a copy shop, if necessary. *Reminder: The rectangle is longer than the width.*

b. Appliqué the rickrack to the dress by stitching in place or using a small amount of fusible web. (Press the rickrack to a piece of fusible web, remove the paper backing, and cut away the excess web.)

c. Using a # 4 pencil, trace the embroidery detail onto the appliqué blocks. Thread your # 8 embroidery needle with 1 strand of floss. Use the stem stitch to complete the embroidery designs. See Embroidery Stitches (page 15).

2. Assemble the quilt center through the inner border, referring to the quilt layout.

3. Appliqué the leaves and circle flowers onto the inner quilt borders.

4. Add the outer borders and corner blocks. Appliqué flowers and buttons will be added after the quilt is finished.

5. Refer to pages 12–14 for finishing details.

Quilting Suggestion

This quilt was machine quilted in the ditch and in a meandering fashion in the quilt center and borders.

Final Touches—Dimensional Flowers:

Make 10 dimensional flowers and attach them to the quilt by placing a button in the middle of each flower and stitching it onto the quilt. Refer to the quilt photo, page 40, for placement.

1. For each flower, select 2 different fabrics and cut 1 square for each, 3½" x 3½".

2. From the fusible web cut a square, 3½" x 3½".

3. Place the fusible web onto the wrong side of one of the fabric squares, rough side of web down, and press. Remove the paper backing.

4. With wrong sides facing, press the 2 fabric squares together.

5. Make a paper template of the flower design on page 44.

6. Place the paper template onto the fused squares and trace around it. Cut out the flower shape.

7. Repeat, using different fabric combinations, for a total of 10 flowers.

8. Arrange the flowers around the outer border. Place a button in the center of each and sew to the quilt through the button.

QUILTED KNITTING TOTE FOR SUE
18" x 18"

Quilted Knitting Tote
for SUE

Sunbonnet Sue has always been known for her industrious nature. Surely, knitting must have been one of her endeavors. Featuring Sue plying her needles, this ample knitting tote pays stylish tribute to this icon of feminine energy.

QUILTED KNITTING TOTE FOR SUE 19" x 19"

Supply List:

Note: Yardage is based on fabric that is at least 40" wide.

1⅛ yds. print fabric for front borders, back, and straps

Fat quarter light background fabric for embroidery

¼ yd. inner border fabric

Cotton batting 24" wide x 1¼ yds.

¾ yd. muslin for backing

¾ yd. lining fabric

2 skeins embroidery floss to coordinate with print fabric

Embroidery needle #7 or 8

Extra hard pencil for tracing design onto background fabric

Package of jumbo rickrack (at least 1 yd.) to match the embroidery floss

Cutting Measurements

I always cut my background a little larger than called for because the stitching may shrink the background slightly. Trim the piece to size after the stitching is complete.

Light Background

1 rectangle, 7½" x 9½"

Inner Border

2 strips, 1½" x 7½" (top and bottom)
2 strips, 1½" x 11½" (sides)

Outer Border, Tote Back, Straps (Print fabric)

1 outer border strip, 3" x 9½" (top)
1 outer border strip, 5" x 9½" (bottom)
2 outer border strips, 5" x 19½" (sides)
1 square, 19½" x 19½" (tote back)
2 strips, 3" x 34" (shoulder straps)

Batting

2 squares, 19½" x 19½"
2 strips, 1" x 34" (shoulder straps)

Muslin

2 squares, 19½" x 19½"

Lining

2 squares, 19½" x 19½"

Rickrack

2 strips of rickrack, 7½" (top and bottom)
2 strips of rickrack, 9½" (sides)

Directions:

Use ½" seam allowances unless otherwise noted.

1. Sew the embroidery design (page 52) onto the background fabric:

a. Using the extra hard pencil, trace the design onto the light background rectangle.

b. Thread the embroidery needle with 2 strands of embroidery floss. Use the stem stitch to complete the designs. See Embroidery Stitches, page 15.

c. Press the completed embroidery on the wrong side.

2. Add the borders:

a. Baste the shorter rickrack strips to the top and bottom of the embroidered center. Position the rickrack so that ½ will show after the inner border is sewn. Baste the longer rickrack strips to the sides of the embroidered center, in the same manner.

b. Stitch the shorter inner border strips to the top and bottom of the embroidered center, catching the rickrack. Repeat on the sides, using the longer inner border strips and rickrack. Press.

c. Sew the top and bottom outer borders to the center block, making sure the 3" border is at the top and the 5" border is at the bottom. Sew the side outer borders (Fig. 1). Press the completed tote front.

3. Quilt the tote front and back:

a. Make a sandwich of the front by layering a muslin square on the bottom, a batting square in the middle, and the tote front on top, face up.

b. Baste and machine or hand quilt. Layer, baste, and quilt the tote back using the remaining 19½" square of muslin, batting, and print fabric.

4. Construct the tote:

a. With right sides together, stitch the sides and the bottom of the tote together. Trim away the seam allowances at the bottom corners (Fig. 2).

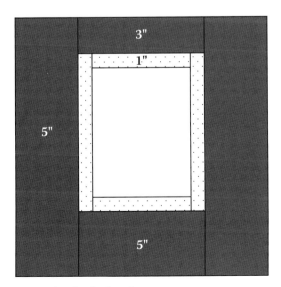

Fig. 1. Apply the borders.

Fig. 2. Trim away the seam allowance.

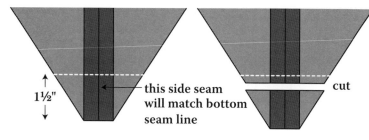

Fig. 3. Cut away each corner.

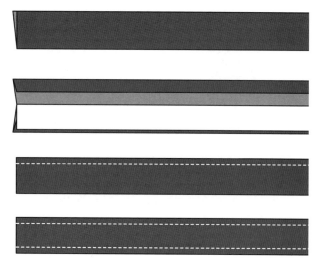

Fig. 4. Fold the straps and place 1" batting strips inside. Then stitch the edges.

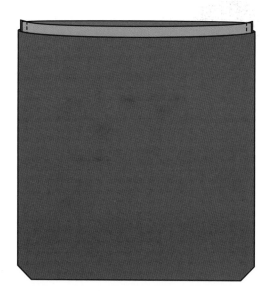

Fig. 5. Place lining inside the tote.

b. To make the bottom of the tote box-shaped, fold the tote at the seam lines, matching the bottom seam at the side seams. Pin the side seams and the bottom seam together, 1½" above each corner. Stitch across each corner as shown in figure 3. Cut away each corner and turn the tote right side out.

c. Referring to figure 4, make 2 straps by folding each 3" x 34" strip in half, lengthwise, wrong side together. Press. Turn in the fabric strips ½" on each outside edge and press. Place 1" batting strips inside the folded straps, at the fold line. Pin the edges together and stitch close to the edge. Stitch the opposite edge inside the fold line. Set the straps aside.

d. Make the tote lining by placing the 2 lining squares right sides together. Using a ⅜" seam allowance, stitch the squares together at the sides and bottom edge. (The ⅜" seam allowance will adjust for the thickness of the quilted tote, allowing the lining to fit more smoothly.) Stitch across the corners of the lining as you did with the tote. Trim away the corners.

e. Referring to figure 5, place the lining inside the tote, wrong sides together and matching seams. Align the top edges of the lining and the tote. Turn in the top edges of the tote and lining inward ½", concealing the raw edges between the tote and the lining. Baste the tote and the lining together, along the edge of the folded seam allowance.

f. Insert the straps. Measure in 3½" from each side seam of the tote front and back.

Snip the basting stitches 1½" toward the center of the tote at these 4 places.

Slip the strap ends to extend ½" between the tote and the lining at these points and re-baste the tote and lining, catching in the straps at these 4 points.

g. Stitch close to the top edge of the tote. Stitch again ¼" from the previous stitching.

Happy Knitting!

B. Alderman 1/07

SUNBONNET PAPER DOLL QUILT
30½" x 33½"

SUNBONNET *Paper Doll Quilt*

Little girls growing up in the 1930s and '40s could find hours worth of entertainment with a 10 cent book of paper dolls. My personal favorites were movie star paper dolls: Shirley Temple, June Allison, Dale Evans, to name a few. They all had beautiful clothes, of course, and it was fun to cut out each outfit and fit it to the paper doll. Come to think of it, I still love scissor cutting and I still love clothes. I wonder where that came from!

Here is little Sunbonnet Sue with her cute paper doll wardrobe, just waiting for you to put it all together in a wee quilt for the special little girl in your life.

SUNBONNET PAPER DOLL QUILT
30½" x 33½"

Supply List

Note: Yardage is based on fabric that is at least 40" wide.

1 yd. white-on-white background and inner border fabric
¼ yd. middle border and appliqué fabric
⅞ yd. outer border, binding and appliqué fabric
Additional scraps for appliqué
1½ yds. lightweight, paper-backed, fusible web
Black machine thread for finishing appliqué by machine or
Black embroidery floss for finishing appliqué by hand
34" x 37" batting
34" x 37" backing – 1 yd.

Cutting Measurements

I always cut my background a little larger than called for because the appliqué and stitching may shrink the background slightly. Trim the pieces to size after the stitching is complete.

CENTER BACKGROUND

1 rectangle, 15½" x 18½"

INNER BACKGROUND BORDER

2 strips, 3¾" x 15½" (top and bottom)
2 strips, 3¾" x 25" (sides)

MIDDLE BORDERS

2 strips, 1¼" x 22" (top and bottom)
2 strips, 1¼" x 26½" (sides)

OUTER BORDER

2 strips, 4" x 23½" (top and bottom)
2 strips, 4" x 33½" (sides)

BINDING

4 strips, 1⅛" x 40"

SUNBONNET PAPER DOLL QUILT layout

Directions

1. Appliqué the Sunbonnet Sue paper doll designs (pages 57–59) to the center background rectangle:

a. Using the method you prefer or referring to the Directions for Fusible-Web Appliqué (pages 10–12), appliqué the paper doll appliqué pieces onto the center background rectangle.

b. Arrange the flower designs in a pleasing way and appliqué onto the background.

2. Inner background border:

a. Appliqué the scissors shapes onto the inner border strips.

b. Sew the borders to the quilt, top and bottom first, then sides.

3. Remaining borders: Sew each border to the quilt top and bottom first, then sides.

4. Refer pages 12–14 for finishing details.

Quilting Suggestion

This quilt was quilted by machine in the ditch. The center and borders were quilted in a meandering fashion.

SWEET PEAS AND PANSIES
47" x 47"

Precious Sunbonnet *Quilts* ∗ *Betty Alderman*

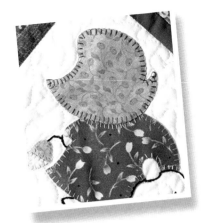

Sweet Peas and Pansies

This quilt, SWEET PEAS AND PANSIES, is a tribute to Bertha Corbett, who created the original Sunbonnet Babies more than 100 years ago. Bertha was a talented artist who surrounded herself with all the things she loved; among her favorites were sweet peas and pansies. Those of us who admire this gifted artist should think of Bertha Corbett whenever we see a lovely flower or a winsome baby. Her art has helped us to remember a time when wholesomeness was a virtue we sought and treasured.

SWEET PEAS AND PANSIES
Approximately 47" x 47"

Supply List

Note: Yardage is based on fabric that is at least 40" wide.

1 yd. light background fabric

¾ yd. 1st light green print for sashing, 1st border and appliqué

¾ yd. 2nd light green print for sashing and appliqué

¼ yd. 1st dark green print for sashing

1¾ yds. 2nd dark green print for sashing and outer border

6 different ½ yd. cuts of purple prints for piecing, binding, and appliqué

2 different ½ yd. cuts of green prints for piecing and appliqué

Scrap of pink fabric for Sweet Pea appliqué

Machine threads to match fabrics for finishing appliqué by machine or

Embroidery floss for finishing by hand

1 skein yellow DMC® embroidery floss

2 skeins black DMC embroidery floss

1 yd. of lightweight, paper-backed fusible web for machine appliqué

55" x 55" batting

55" x 55" backing – 3 yds.

Cutting Measurements

I always cut my background a little larger than called for because the appliqué and stitching may shrink the background slightly. Trim the pieces to size after the stitching is complete.

BACKGROUND
12 squares, 6½" x 6½"

SASHING (EACH OF 1ST AND 2ND LIGHT GREEN PRINTS)

4 strips, 1¾" x width of fabric

SASHING (EACH OF 1ST AND 2ND DARK GREEN PRINTS)

4 strips, 1" x width of fabric

CORNER TRIANGLES (FROM EACH OF 4 DIFFERENT PURPLES)

1 square, 13⅛" x 13⅛". Cut each of the 4 squares once diagonally to yield 2 triangles per square. Use one triangle of each print for corners of the quilt. Use the leftover fabric for appliqué.

SIDE SETTING TRIANGLES (FROM EACH OF 2 REMAINING PURPLES AND 2 REMAINING GREEN PRINTS)

1 square, 12½" x 12½". Cut each of 4 squares twice diagonally to yield 4 triangles per square. Use one triangle of each print for middle setting triangles along the side of the quilt. Use the leftover fabric for appliqué.

INNER BORDER (1ST LIGHT GREEN PRINT)

4 strips 1" x width of fabric

OUTER BORDER (2ND DARK GREEN PRINT)

4 strips 6" x 50" along the length of the fabric

BINDING

6 strips, 1⅛" x 40"

Directions

1. Appliqué the blocks with embroidery:

a. Using the method you prefer or refer-ring to the Directions for Fusible-Web Appliqué (pages 10–12), appliqué the Sunbonnet designs (page 64) onto 6 background squares. Appliqué the Pansy pattern (page 65) on the remaining 6 background squares. Note that the background square is "on point."

b. Referring to the Embroidery Stitches (page 15), add embroidery detail to the appliqué with a stem stitch.

2. Sashing:

a. Sew the 1st dark green 1" strip to the 1st light green 1¾" strip, along the lengthwise edges. The sewn strip set should measure 2¼" wide. Make a total of 4 strip-sets.

b. Cut these strip-sets into 16 pieces, each 2¼" x 6½". These are to be used as sashing between the appliqué blocks.

c. Sew the 2nd dark green 1" strip to the 2nd light green 1¾" strip in the same manner as step a. Make a total of 4 strip-sets.

d. Cut 3 of these strip-sets to measure 33¼" long and cut the remaining strip into 2 strips, each measuring 17¾" long. These 5 strips are also to be used for sashing between the appliqué blocks.

3. Complete the quilt center:

a. Referring to the quilt layout on page 63, assemble the quilt center.

b. Appliqué the bow designs onto the corner triangles.

4. Adding the borders:

a. Determine mea-surement

to cut the exact length of the border strips:

• For top and bottom borders which will be joined first, measure across the center of the quilt from side to side and cut 2 border strips to this measurement. Join border strips to the top and bottom of the quilt.

• For side borders measure from top to bottom across the center of the quilt and cut 2 border strips to this measurement. Join border strips to the sides of the quilt

• For additional borders, repeat this method for each border and join to the quilt before moving on to the next border.

b. Add the inner border first then the outer border.

5. Appliqué the leaf and heart motifs onto the borders, referring to the quilt picture.

6. Refer to pages 12–14 for finishing details.

SWEET PEAS AND PANSIES *quilt layout*

Quilting Suggestion

Diane Ebner finished this quilt with machine quilting in the ditch. She stitched a meandering pattern in both the background and outside border.

SLEEPY TIME SUE
30½" x 31½"

Precious Sunbonnet Quilts ✳ *Betty Alderman*

Sleepy Time Sue

I wonder, sometimes, how many Sunbonnet quilts have been made and how many have been tucked around sleepy little girls at night. It seemed appropriate to design a quilt featuring a little Sunbonnet girl in her nightgown, lighting her way to dreamland.

Sleepy Time Sue
30" x 31½"

Supply List:

Note: Yardage is based on fabric that is at least 40" wide.

- ½ yd. floral fabric for five of the blocks
- ¼ yd. light background fabric for Sunbonnet appliqué
- ¾ yd. border fabric
- ¼ yd. binding and appliqué fabric
- ⅛ yd. print for wavy detail on the top and bottom border
- ¼ yd. binding and appliqué fabric
- 5–8 different scraps for Sunbonnet appliqué
- Black and flesh-colored scraps for hands and shoes

Machine thread for finishing the appliqué by machine or
Embroidery floss for hand finishing the appliqué
3 yds. ⅝" grosgrain ribbon
1½ yd. ⅜" grosgrain ribbon
38" x 39" batting
38" x 39" backing – 1⅛ yds.

Cutting Measurements

I always cut my background a little larger than called for because the appliqué and stitching may shrink the background slightly. Trim the pieces to size after the stitching is complete.

Floral fabric block
5 rectangles, 8" x 8½"

Background
4 rectangles, 8" x 8½"

Border
2 strips, 4" x 23" (top and bottom)
2 strips, 4" x 31½" (sides)

Binding
4 strips, 1⅛" x 40"

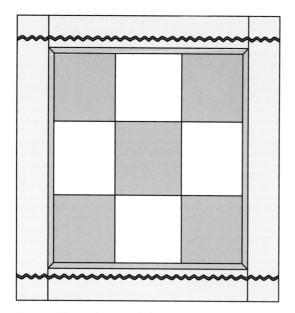

SLEEPY TIME SUE quilt layout

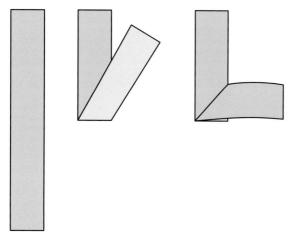

⅝" *ribbon, corner detail*

Directions:

1. Appliqué the Sunbonnet Sue designs (page 69) on the background rectangles.

Using the method you prefer or referring to the Directions for Fusible-Web Appliqué (pages 10–12), appliqué the sunbonnet figures onto the background rectangles. *Reminder: the rectangles are longer than the width.*

2. Assemble the quilt as shown in the quilt layout.

3. Create and appliqué the wavy detail onto the top and bottom borders. See the quilt photo, page 66, for placement.

4. Stitch the ⅝" ribbon onto the border at the seam between the blocks and borders. The ribbon is sewn at the edge of the blocks onto the border. Both sides of the ribbon are sewn down. See the adjacent figure for corner detail.

5. From the ⅜" ribbon, make 4 bows and attach them at the top of each appliqué block.

6. Refer to pages 12–14 for finishing details.

Quilting Suggestion

This quilt was machine quilted around each figure. The background was quilted in a meandering pattern.

Good Morning, Good Night Pillows
15" x 15"

Good Morning, Good Night
Pillows

Devotees of Redwork have probably seen numerous examples of antique linens with "Good Morning" and "Good Night" embroidered on them. Here is my version of that bygone whimsy from the nineteenth century.

Good Morning, Good Night Pillows
2 pillows, each 15" x 15"

Supply List for 2 Pillows:

Note: Yardage is based on fabric that is at least 40" wide.

½ yd. white background fabric

1¼ yds. pillow print

½ yd. muslin

18" x 36" batting

2 packages coordinating jumbo rickrack
   (3 yards)

3 skeins red embroidery floss, DMC 498

2 purchased 15" pillow forms

Embroidery needle, # 7 or 8

Extra hard pencil

Cutting Measurements for 2 Pillows:

I always cut my background a little larger than called for because the appliqué and stitching may shrink the background slightly. Trim the piece to size after the stitching is complete.

Background fabric

2 squares, 9½" x 9½"

Print fabric

4 strips, 3½" x 9½" for top and bottom border strips

4 strips, 3½" x 15½" for side border strips

4 rectangles, 12" x 15½" for the pillow backs

Muslin

2 squares, 15½" x 15½"

Batting

2 squares, 15½" x 15½"

Rickrack

4 pieces, 9½" long

4 pieces, 15½" long

Directions

Make 2 pillows.

Use ¼" seam allowance unless otherwise noted.

1. Sew the embroidery designs (pages 74–75) onto the background fabric:

a. Use the extra hard pencil to trace each design onto the white background squares.

b. Thread the embroidery needle with 2 strands of embroidery floss. Use the stem stitch to complete the designs. See Embroidery Stitches, page 15.

c. Press each completed block on the wrong side.

2. Add the borders:

a. Baste the shorter rickrack strips to the top and bottom edges of the embroidered square; center of the rickrack should be ¼" from the raw edge of the square so that half of the rickrack will show when the borders are sewn on.

b. Stitch the shorter print border strips to the top and bottom of the embroidered center, catching in the rickrack. Press the seams towards the border and the rickrack towards the center. Repeat on the side edges, using the longer rickrack strips and borders.

3. Quilt the pillow tops:

a. Layer a muslin square on the bottom, batting in the middle, and the completed pillow front, face up, on top.

b. Baste the layers together and quilt by hand or machine. Repeat with the other pillow front, batting, and muslin square.

4. Make the pillow backs:

a. Fold 1" along one long edge of each of the 4 pillow back rectangles and press. Turn under again and press. Stitch close to the folded edge through all layers as shown.

b. For each pillow, lay 2 pillow backs right side up. Hemmed edges are at the center. Overlap the hemmed edges, making a square, 15½" x 15½". Baste the overlap close to the raw edges.

5. Construct the pillows:

a. With right sides together, place the pillow front onto the pillow back. Stitch around the pillow on all 4 sides, using ¼" seams.

b. Clip the corners, turn and press. Insert pillow forms into the pillows.

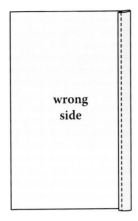

Fig. 4a. *Stitch through all layers, close to the folded edge.*

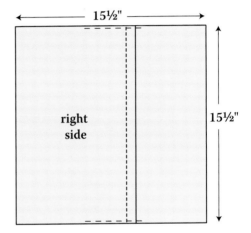

Fig. 4b. *Baste the overlap close to the raw edges making a 15½" square.*

GOOD MORNING, GOOD NIGHT pillows layout

Good morning

GOODBYE TO SUMMER
36" x 37½"

Precious Sunbonnet Quilts ∗ *Betty Alderman*

Goodbye to SUMMER

On a golden fall day, Sunbonnet Sue waves goodbye to summer. She soon will be trading her sunbonnet for a warm and snug chapeau. Many of the buttons I added to the flowers were the type used on winter coats in the 1930s and '40s. Brrrr! Just a hint of what is to come.

GOODBYE TO SUMMER
36" x 37½"

Supply List:

Note: Yardage is based on fabric that is at least 40" wide.

1¾ yds. background and border fabric

¾ yd. sashing and binding fabric

8–12 different scraps, for appliqué,
  Flying Geese, and sashing squares

3 yds. lightweight, paper-backed fusible web

Thread to match fabrics for finishing appliqué
  by machine or

Matching embroidery floss for finishing
  appliqué by hand

28 large vintage buttons for flower centers

40" x 42" batting

40" x 42" backing – 1¼ yds.

Cutting Measurements

I always cut my background a little larger than called for because the appliqué and stitching may shrink the background slightly. Trim the pieces to size after the stitching is complete.

BACKGROUND

9 rectangles, 8" x 8½"

SASHING

12 strips, 1½" x 8" (between blocks – horizontal)

12 strips, 1½" x 8½" (between blocks – vertical)

SASHING CORNER SQUARES – FABRIC VARIETY

16 squares, 1½" x 1½"

BORDER

2 strips, 5" x 27"

2 strips, 5" x 28½"

FLYING GEESE BORDER CORNER BLOCKS – FABRIC VARIETY

8 rectangles, 5" x 2¾"

FLYING GEESE BORDER CORNER BLOCKS – BACKGROUND

16 squares, 2¾" x 2¾"

BINDING

5 strips, 1⅛" x 40"

Directions

1. Appliqué Sunbonnet Sue designs (pages 80–81) to the background rectangles. Using the method you prefer or referring to the Directions for Fusible-Web Appliqué (pages 10–12), appliqué the sunbonnet designs onto the 9 background rectangles. *Reminder: The rectangle is longer than the width.*

2. Assemble the center of the quilt as shown in the quilt layout.

3. Appliqué the flowers, stems and leaves, evenly spaced, onto the border strips. Refer to the picture of the quilt as a guide.

4. Make 8 units to assemble into 4 Flying Geese corner blocks:

a. To make one unit, place one 2¾" background square on one end of a 5" x 2¾" rectangle, right sides together. Stitch as shown. (Fig. 1a.)

b. Trim the two bottom corners away. (Fig. 1b.)

c. Fold and press the top triangle back as shown. (Fig. 1c.)

d. Repeat on the opposite end of the rectangle to make one unit. (Fig. 1d.) Stitch 4 pairs of units together to complete 4 Flying Geese blocks 5" square.

5. Sew the borders and corner Flying Geese blocks to the quilt:

a. Stitch the top and bottom borders to the quilt center.

b. Stitch the Flying Geese blocks to each end of the 2 side borders. Note the direction of each Flying Geese block. Stitch these borders to the sides of the quilt.

6. Refer to pages 12–14 for finishing details.

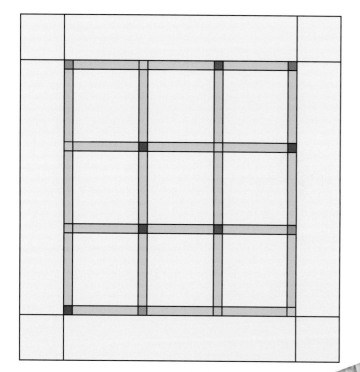

***Goodbye to Summer* quilt layout**

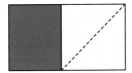

Fig. 1a.

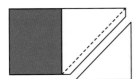

Fig. 1b.

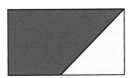

Fig. 1c.

Fig. 1d.

Quilting Suggestion

This quilt was quilted by hand, in the ditch and echo quilted around the figures. The borders were quilted in the ditch and ¼" away from the appliqué. As a final touch, sew buttons in the center of the each flower.

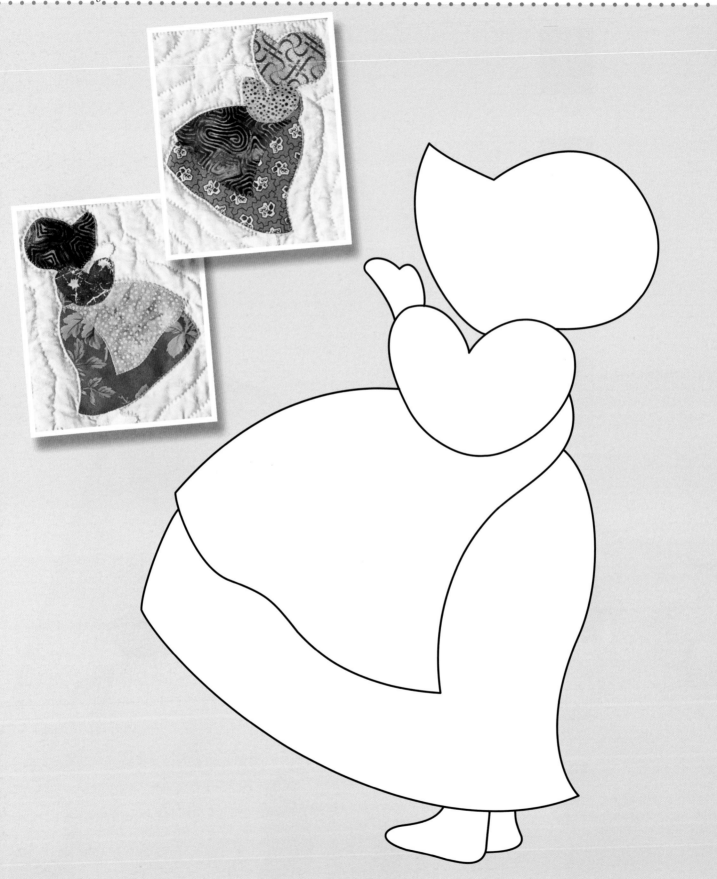

HALLOWEEN PUMPKINS
27½" x 31½"

Halloween Pumpkins

What better time than Halloween to pair the reds and blues from your fabric stash with those frightening yellows and oranges that seem to scare us all. Sunbonnet Sue and her black kitty pull it all together in the pumpkin patch.

HALLOWEEN PUMPKIN
27½" x 31½"

Supply List:

Note: Yardage is based on fabric that is at least 40" wide.

1 yd. light tan fabric for background blocks
    and outer border
⅛ yd. yellow and orange for pumpkins
Scrap of flesh-colored fabric for hands
1½ yds. lightweight, paper-backed fusible web
Fat eighth, black fabric for kittens, bonnets,
    and shoes
2 skeins of black embroidery floss
¾ yd. red print fabric for apron, inner border,
    and binding
½ yd. blue print fabric for dress and border
    appliqué
32" x 36" batting
32" x 36" backing – 1 yd.

Cutting Measurements

I always cut my background a little larger than called for because the appliqué and stitching may shrink the background slightly. Trim the pieces to size after the stitching is complete.

BACKGROUND

4 rectangles, 8½" x 10½"

INNER BORDER

2 strips, 2" x 16½" top and bottom
2 strips, 2" x 23½" sides

OUTER BORDER

2 strips, 4½" x 19½"
2 strips, 4½" x 31½"

BINDING

4 strips, 1⅛" x 40"

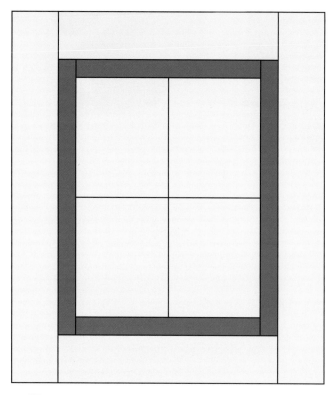

HALLOWEEN PUMPKINS *quilt layout*

Directions

1. Appliqué:

a. Using the method you prefer or referring to the Directions for Fusible-Web Appliqué (pages 10–12), appliqué the Sunbonnet Sue, kitty and pumpkin designs (pages 86–87) onto the 4 background rectangles. Refer to the quilt photograph (page 82) for placement.

b. Appliqué the vine design onto the side border strips. Add the center motifs to the top and bottom border strips.

c. Thread an embroidery needle with 2 strands of black embroidery floss and do a running stitch around the outside edge of all the appliquéd pieces. Refer to Embroidery Stitches (page 15).

2. Assemble the quilt, referring to the layout and the picture.

3. Refer to pages 12–14 for finishing details.

Quilting Suggestion

Using threads that matched the fabrics, this quilt was entirely machine quilted. Each appliqué was detail quilted. The light tan background was then quilted in the ditch around the inner border. The center background was quilted in a meandering fashion and the border was echo quilted around the appliqué.

reverse here for side motif

reverse here for
top and bottom motif

border appliqué
for HALLOWEEN PUMPKINS

SUNBONNETS AROUND THE BLOCK
66½" x 66½"

SUNBONNETS Around the Block

While the other quilts in this book are primarily appliqué, I thought it would be nice to include a larger quilt that appealed to those of you who like to piece, as well. Nine blocks, named Around the Block, make up the center portion but never fear, Sunbonnets make their appearance on the border. I call my quilt SUNBONNETS AROUND THE BLOCK, because growing up I lived in a neighborhood where most of my friends lived "around the block."

Although the supply list and the directions specify a pink and blue colorway for easy clarification, any pleasing color combination will work.

SUNBONNETS AROUND THE BLOCK
66½" x 66½"

Supply List:

Note: Yardage is based on fabric that is at least 40" wide.

½ yd. pink print for inner border
2 yds. white for outer border, cut lengthwise
½ yd. dark blue for binding
1 yd. total of a variety of dark blue prints
1 yd. total of a variety of light blue prints
1½ yds. total of a variety of dark pink prints
1½ yds. total of a variety of light pink prints
1½ yds. lightweight, paper-backed fusible web for appliqué
74" x 74" batting
74" x 74" backing – 4⅛ yds.
Fine line, black permanent pen
Flesh-colored crayon
Thread for piecing
Machine embroidery thread to match appliqué fabric for finishing appliqué by machine or
Embroidery floss to match appliqué fabric for finishing appliqué by hand

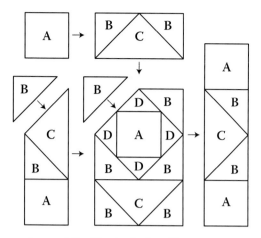

Around the Block piecing diagram

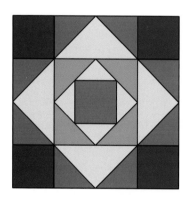

Color layouts for blocks

Cutting Measurements:

You will be making 9 Around the Block, 16" blocks using a different combination of fabrics in each block. I suggest that you study the photo and the color quilt layout to help you decide which fabrics and values to use. Notice that by strategically placing dark blue prints in particular areas of the center and corner blocks, a secondary, square-in-a-square design appears.

Using the Around the Block templates, pages 92–93, cut the required number of pieces for each block.

INNER BORDER

2 strips, 2" x 48½" (top and bottom)
2 strips, 2" x 51 ½" (sides)

OUTER BORDER

2 strips, 8" x 51½" (top and bottom)
2 strips, 8" x 66½" (sides)

BINDING

8 strips, 1⅛" x 40"

Directions:

1. Construct the quilt blocks:

a. Referring to the Around the Block piecing diagram and the color block layouts on this page, piece the 9 blocks.

b. Referring to the quilt layout, page 91, assemble the quilt center of 9 pieced blocks.

2. Add the inner border, top and bottom first, then the side borders.

3. Outer border appliqué:

a. Fuse and appliqué the Sunbonnet figures (page 94) evenly along each border. The top of each figure should be placed 1½" from the edge of the border strip. You should leave approximately 5" from arm to arm to allow space for the swag.

b. Appliqué the swags in place. The corner figures and corner swags will be appliquéd after the borders are attached.

c. Using the black permanent pen, trace the shoes and hands onto the borders. Blacken the shoes with the pen and color the hands with the flesh-colored crayon. Heat-set the pen and crayon work with a warm iron.

4. Add the outer border, top and bottom first, then side borders.

5. Appliqué the corner figures and swags. Finish with shoes and hands.

6. Refer to pages 12–14 for finishing details.

SUNBONNETS AROUND THE BLOCK quilt layout

Quilting Suggestion

This quilt was beautifully and creatively quilt-ed on a longarm quilting machine by Kathleen York. She used pink thread in the pieced center of the quilt and white thread in the borders.

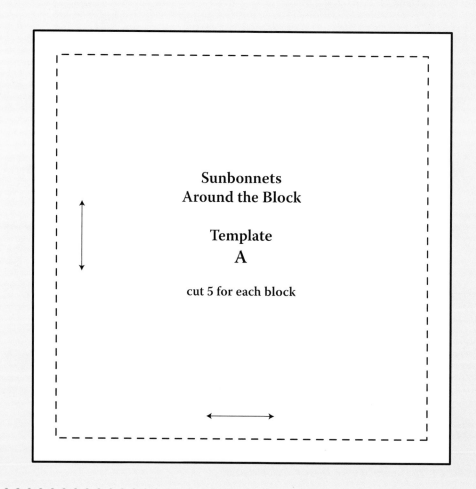

**Sunbonnets
Around the Block**

**Template
A**

cut 5 for each block

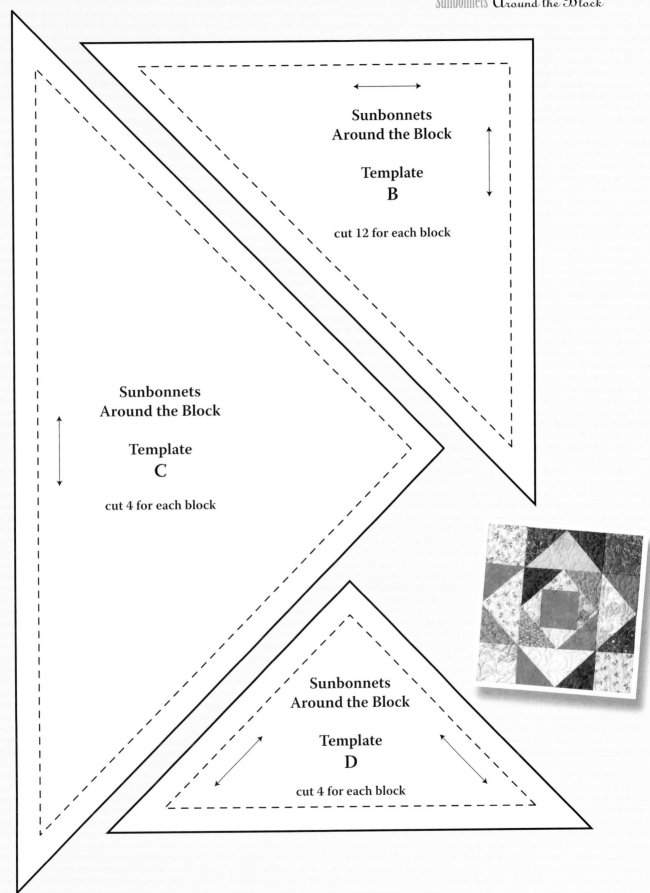

**Sunbonnets
Around the Block**

**Template
B**

cut 12 for each block

**Sunbonnets
Around the Block**

**Template
C**

cut 4 for each block

**Sunbonnets
Around the Block**

**Template
D**

cut 4 for each block

About the AUTHOR

Betty Alderman has been designing and publishing her patterns under her own name since 1992. Designing and making quilts is the perfect fit for Betty as she has a background in fine arts and has had a passion for sewing and "making things" since she was a child.

Most of her designs are applique or embroidery or a combination of both. In addition to publishing her own patterns, she has two books published by AQS, *Favorite Redwork Designs* and *Favorite Appliqué and Embroidery Quilts*. When time permits, she teaches and does trunk shows throughout the United States.

Mother of three grown children and grandmother of six, Betty resides in Palmyra, New York, with her husband, Fred.

Other AQS Books

This is only a small selection of the books available from the American Quilter's Society. AQS books are known worldwide for timely topics, clear writing, beautiful color photos, and accurate illustrations and patterns. The following books are available from your local bookseller, quilt shop, or public library.

#7602   us$26.95

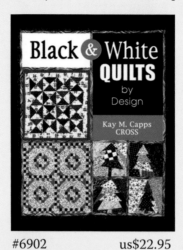

#6902   us$22.95

#7600   us$26.95

#7073   us$24.95

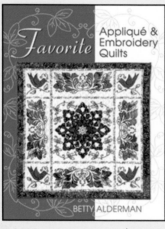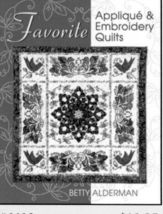

#6410   us$19.95

#7489   us$24.95

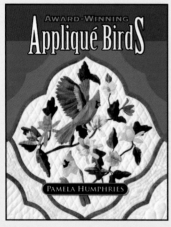

#7494   us$21.95

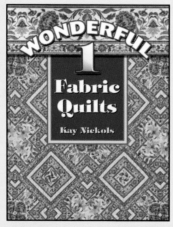

#7487   us$19.95

#7486   us$22.95